Phonics Poetry
Teaching Word Families

Timothy V. Rasinski
Kent State University

Belinda S. Zimmerman
Walls Elementary School
Kent, Ohio

Allyn and Bacon
Boston   London   Toronto   Sydney   Tokyo   Singapore

Series editor: Aurora Martinez Ramos
Series editorial assistant: Beth Slater
Marketing manager: Stephen Smith

Copyright © 2001 by Allyn & Bacon
A Pearson Education Company
160 Gould Street
Needham Heights, MA 02494

Internet: www.abacon.com

Library of Congress Cataloging-in-Publication Data
Rasinski, Timothy V.
   Phonics poetry : teaching word families / Timothy V. Rasinski, Belinda S. Zimmerman.
      p. cm.
   Includes index.
   ISBN 0-205-30909-7
      1. Reading--Phonetic method. 2. Poetry--Study and teaching. I. Zimmerman, Belinda
S. II. Title.

LB1573.3 .R37 2001
372.45'5--dc21   00-063946

Printed in the United States of America

10   9   8   7   6   5   4   04

Contents

iv

Preface

Throughout the country, many teachers are recognizing the value and utility of teaching phonics and word recognition through the use of *phonograms* (also known as *word families* or *rimes*). Research tends to validate the confidence that teachers have placed in teaching phonics through phonograms—it works! This book represents an extension on the ways that phonograms have been used in phonics instruction. What distinguishes the approach recommended in this book from many of the rest is the comprehensiveness and intensity to which we employ phonograms.

In many classrooms, teachers teach phonograms by introducing individual phonograms and the speech sound that each phonogram represents. This is followed by brainstorming words that contain the targeted phonogram. The words may be listed on a large sheet of chart paper and put on display for the entire class to see. Over the next several days, students may practice the words and add new words to the chart. After several days of practice and display, the chart is retired and the class moves on to another phonogram.

Although this is a good start in the teaching of phonograms, we think it is only a beginning. Words that students can identify quickly in isolation may not be so easy in the context of authentic reading, such as stories, essays, reports, and poems. The next step in the teaching of phonograms is to get the students reading and rereading words that contain the targeted phonograms in authentic texts. And, what kind of text, by its very nature, is brief yet contains several (rhyming) words containing the targeted phonogram? Yes, poetry!

In her article on the timing and teaching of phonograms, Francine Johnston (1999) stated:

> The thoughtful use of materials with a high percentage of words with the same patterns as those taught in phonics lessons makes sense as it increases the chance that children will make connections between the teacher-directed study of word families and their own encounters with words in meaningful contexts. (p. 70)

We advocate moving students directly into multiple readings of short, highly predictable, patterned, rhythmical, enjoyable rhyming poems. Students read and reread the short poems until they can read with some degree of fluency. Then, once the poem is mastered and enjoyed, instructional focus begins to shift to lines, phrases, words within the poem, and letter patterns within the words. Thus, in this whole-to-part process, students develop an understanding that it is the meaning of the whole text that matters, but that access to the text is facilitated by knowledge of phrasing, words, and letter patterns.

Although many teachers agree that the use of rhyming poems in teaching phonograms is a valuable approach, a common complaint issued by some teachers is that they do not have easy access to the poems that they can use to teach the phonograms in an ongoing and systematic way. Thus, the idea for this book was born.

At its heart, *Phonics Poetry* is essentially a collection of poems that can be used to teach and practice phonograms, the phonics element that appears to have great promise in helping students become proficient decoders.

How This Book Is Organized

Edward Fry (1998) found over 300 different phonograms that could be taught in a phonics program. That is a fairly large number—certainly a number that could not easily be covered in a school year. However, Fry's analysis of phonograms identified the 38 most common word families. This list of 38 phonograms can be employed to decode 654 single-syllable words. He suggests that this list of 38 phonograms may be a useful guide in assisting teachers and curriculum developers in deciding which phonograms to teach as soon as possible.

This reasoning makes sense to us—teach the phonograms that will be of greatest usefulness to readers as they work to sound out words they encounter in their reading. Thus, we use the 38 phonograms identified by Fry (1998) as the organizing principle for this book (see the table on page 5). Each of the 38 phonograms is represented by at least two poems. Each poem contains two or more words reflecting a particular phonogram and, in many cases, more than one phonogram.

In addition to the poems themselves, we have included a handy, easy-to-use table that identifies the most common phonograms and the poems that can be used to provide critical practice in poetry reading and phonogram learning. Once you select the phonogram you wish to teach at a particular time, you can consult the organizing table to identify those poems and rhymes that correspond to the targeted phonogram (see pages 164–167).

We have also included, with each poem, other suggestions for extending students' reading and word learning. These include, among others, word bank and word sort activities (letters enclosed by forward slashes should be read as "sound of"; for example, /s/ = "sound of *s*"), cloze sentences (sentences with targeted words deleted), group poetry writing ideas, brainstorming activities, word analogies, and related children's trade books.

In the Introduction of this book, we will suggest ways in which you may wish to use the poems with your students. These suggestions are based on our own work with students. However, please remember that our intention in developing this book is not to prescribe a set of activities that you must feel compelled to implement with your students. Rather, we recognize that only you know the needs and interests of your students. We defer to you, the classroom or clinical teacher, the ultimate responsibility for choosing which phonogram to teach and what activities to use in your instruction. This book should be employed as a valuable resource or guide in that endeavor, not a recipe book. We recognize that each teacher has her or his own particular style of instruction. We do not want to dictate to you exactly how these poems should be taught. The important thing is to have fun with poems. Read and reread them throughout the school year. Draw students' attention to the phonograms in each poem. Perhaps even encourage your students to try writing their own rhymes. Poetry, above all, should be fun.

Introduction:
Phonics through Poetry

Let's face it—phonics is an essential part of learning to read for most children. In English, sounds of the language are represented by written letters; for example, the sound of the letter *t*, as in *top*, is always represented by the written letter *t*. Phonics involves learning the written letters that represent sounds. Sounds easy doesn't it? But it doesn't take long to realize that in English the sound-symbol relationships called phonics are not simple at all.

For example, the sound normally associated with *f* can be represented by the letter *f* or by the letter combination *ph*. The "sh" sound, as in *she*, is usually written as an *sh*. However, the "sh" sound is also represented by the written letter *t*, as in *nation*, and in other ways as well. So, different sounds in English can be represented by more than one letter or letter combination.

Similarly, individual letters or letter combinations can represent more than one sound. Again, for example, the written letter *c* can represent the sound of "s," as in *sea*, or the sound "k," as in *kitten*. Combine that *c* with a following *h* and the two letters together make an altogether different sound! As you can see from just these few examples, the individual sounds that can be represented by different letters and the different sounds that can be represented by individual letters make phonics a fairly complex task.

Traditionally, phonics has been taught as a set of rules or generalizations. Perhaps you can remember some of these rules from your own school experience. Perhaps you still teach these rules. One of the most notable and enduring generalizations is the one that goes, "When two vowels go walking, the first one does the talking and it says its name." In other words, when there are two adjacent vowels in a syllable, the long sound of the first vowel is used and the second vowel is not pronounced.

Well, a reading researcher by the name of Theodore Clymer decided to take a closer look at the rules that are used in most phonics programs. He collected the rules and tested them against actual words that children learn in the primary grades in order to see just how often the rules actually led the reader to the correct pronunciation of the word. What he found was a huge surprise to the community of reading scholars and teachers who believed in phonics rules. Many of the phonics rules or generalizations that deal with vowels and the middle of words and syllables actually don't work very well. For example, the "two vowels go walking" rule worked less than 50 percent of the time on words that students encounter in reading. Try out that rule on words such as *thief* and *said* and see what you come up with!

Clymer's study, as well as similar studies conducted by others (Johnston, 1999), found that, in general, less than half of the commonly taught phonics generalizations worked with sufficient frequency to justify using them in instructional programs.

So What to Do?

Does the fact that phonics rules don't work terribly well mean that teachers should give up on phonics as an aid to learning how to read? Of course not. But it does mean that educators need to look for other ways to help children use the sound-symbol relationship embedded in words to help them figure out the words they encounter in their reading.

First of all, let's start with the phonics rules that *do* work. These are the ones that deal with consonants that begin words or syllables. These rules are pretty reliable. When a *p* begins a word or syllable and is followed by a vowel, it almost always represents the "p" sound, as in *top*. Similarly, when *sh* begins a word or syllable and is followed by a vowel, it almost always represents the sound associated with "sh," as in *she*. Even that tricky *c* can be turned into a useful rule. When a *c* begins a word or syllable and is followed by the vowels *e* or *i*, it usually represents the sound associated with *s*, as in *sea*. When a *c* begins a word or syllable and is followed by the vowels *a*, *o*, or *u*, it usually represents the sound associated with *k*, as in *kitten*.

So, the consonant letter-sound relationships at the beginning of words or syllables are pretty good. These types of consonants—consonants that precede the vowel in a syllable—are called *onsets*.

Where the trouble starts is with the vowels as well as consonants that follow the vowel in words and syllables. Fortunately, there is an approach to working with these parts of words that has considerable promise. This approach suggests that rather than rely on unreliable rules, one should be looking for patterns of letters that consistently represent sounds and sound combinations.

The most basic type of patterns that involve vowels are called *rimes, phonograms*, or *word families*. The names all refer to the same syllable patterns—the part of the syllable that contains the vowel and all subsequent consonants after the vowel and within the syllable. For example, the rime in the one-syllable word *cat* is *at*, the phonogram in the word *truck* is *uck*, and the word family in the word *day* is *ay*.

Not only are rimes, phonograms, and word families reasonably consistent in the sounds they represent, they are so prevalent in words that knowledge of just a few word families can help readers pronounce a huge number of words. Edward Fry (1998), for example, found that knowledge of only the 38 most common phonograms can help a reader decode 654 one-syllable words (see the table on page 5). When considering the multisyllabic words that can at least be partially decoded using those same 38 phonograms, the number of decodable words reaches into the several thousands. This clearly demonstrates the power and scope of the use of phonograms as a key focus of study in an effective phonics/decoding program.

Many of today's leading scholars in reading development and reading education advocate a phonics approach that leans heavily on the use of phonograms (e.g., Cunningham, 1995; Goswami & Bryant, 1990; Stahl, 1992; Trieman, 1985). In her seminal book on beginning reading, literacy researcher Marilyn Adams (1990) wrote:

> As coherent psychological units in themselves, the onset and rime are relatively easy to remember and to splice back together. Yet another advantage of exploiting phonograms in decoding instruction is that they provide a means of introducing and exercising many primer words with relative efficiency and this, as we have seen, is in marked contrast to the slowness with which words can be developed through individual letter-sound correspondences. (p. 324)

Similarly, noted reading educators Joanne Vacca, Richard Vacca, and Mary Gove (1995) argued:

> Phonics instruction needs to include the teaching of onset and rimes. Instead of teaching phonics rules, teach children to use onsets and rimes.... We can safely conclude that phonics information is much easier for young readers to acquire when phonograms are taught than when a one-on-one blending process is taught. (p. 287)

Some of the most notable reading programs in the country rely heavily on the use of phonograms. For example, in the highly regarded Benchmark Word Detectives Program, a decoding program used in the Benchmark School—a school dedicated to and noted for teaching struggling readers—instruction in phonograms for key words is an essential element (Gaskins, Downer, Anderson, Cunningham, Gaskins, & Schommer, 1988; Gaskins, Ehri, Cress, O'Hara, & Donelly, 1997). Even in our own reading programs, those at the University Reading Clinic that Tim supervises and in Belinda's primary grade classroom at Walls Elementary, students are successfully taught phonics decoding through the use of phonograms.

How to Use This Book

There is no *one* correct way to use this book. Knowledgeable teachers will find ways to incorporate the poems in this book to supplement phonics they already may be teaching and at the same time help students learn to appreciate and enjoy the rhyme, rhythm, and language play that is part of poetry.

If you already have a phonics program in place that takes advantage of phonograms, then you may select poems from this book that match the phonograms on which you may be working on any given day. The poem can be written on the chalkboard or on chart paper, or transferred to an overhead transparency, to be read, reread, and enjoyed by students.

Once students have read and enjoyed the poem several times—reading the poem chorally, in small groups, and individually—you should draw students' attention to individual words and features within words in the poem that you are using. In particular, you will want to draw students' attention to the words that contain the phonograms that you are working on. Highlight those words with markers, word windows, or in some other manner.

But just don't stop there. Examine high-frequency and/or interesting words that you may find in the poem. Point out other word families that you may have covered earlier. This sort of lesson doesn't have to take long—15 to 20 minutes should be more than enough time to read, study, and enjoy the poem. Be sure to keep the poem posted for students to return to throughout the day. You will find that many students will want to read and reread the poem on their own.

You may also want to make copies of the instructed poem for every student to take home and read to their parents and other family members. Having students practice texts such as these several times is a superb way to develop fluency and word recognition skills. Some teachers have students take their copies of poems home and have anyone who listens to them read sign the back of the copy. Such listeners are called Lucky Listeners, and students often engage in friendly rivalries over who has the most Lucky Listeners for each poem. Remember that practice such as this should have an outcome in performance. So, when you ask students to practice poems at home, be sure to give them an opportunity to perform the poem in school to an audience of classmates, teacher, or others.

If you don't have a phonogram-based phonics program that you are already using, this book can be the foundation of one that you develop on your own. It's fairly simple to develop a program when you know what you want to teach and how, in general, you want to teach it.

We suggest that you use the high-frequency list developed by Fry (1998; see the table on page 5) as a guide for determining which phonograms to teach and their general order of introduction. You may wish to group phonograms into logical sets. For example, we recommend that you group word families by the same short vowel sounds (e.g., *at, am, ag, ack, ank, ap, an*) and long vowel sounds (e.g., *ay, ail, ain, ake*). Work through the short vowel phonograms first, one vowel sound at a time, then work through the long vowel sounds, one at a time (Johnston, 1999). As students begin to develop mastery over phonograms, you may want to compare or contrast the phonograms, first by ending consonants of the same short vowel sound, then by comparing different short vowel phonograms, and finally by comparing and contrasting phonograms with the same written vowel but representing long and short vowel sounds (Johnston, 1999).

The Most Common Phonograms	
1. -ay	20. -ug
2. -ill	21. -op
3. -ip	22. -in
4. -at	23. -an
5. -am	24. -est
6. -ag	25. -ink
7. -ack	26. -ow
8. ank	27. -ew
9. -ick	28. -ore
10. -ell	29. -ed
11. -ot	30. -ab
12. -ing	31. -ob
13. -ap	32. -ock
14. -unk	33. -ake
15. -ail	34. -ine
16. ain	35. -ight
17. -eed	36. -im
18. -y	37. -uck
19. -out	38. -um

(Phonograms are listed in order, beginning with phonograms that are contained in the largest number of one-syllable words—the most common phonograms.)

Remember that there is no one correct sequence for teaching phonograms. Much will depend on your own students. Be sure to take advantage of their personal interests, the items they may bring in to share with classmates, their names, and the poems and other texts that they have learned even before coming to school.

Once you have a general idea of the sequence in which you would like to present the phonograms, the question then becomes the way in which the phonograms should be taught. Again, there is no one way that will work for all teachers and for all children. However, we would like to suggest one general approach that has seemed to work for many children. It is a three-step (day) sequence that we describe here. The approach assumes that students have some knowledge of letters and sounds that are represented by consonants in the beginning parts of words and syllables (onsets).

Day 1. Introduce the targeted phonogram or word family. Write it on chart paper and talk about the sound it represents. Then, work with students to brainstorm words that contain the phonogram and sound. List the words on the chart paper. Practice reading the words several times through. Help students see that each word on the list contains the phonogram and, when pronounced, contains the sound associated with the phonogram. Encourage students to look for other words containing the word family in their own reading and be ready to add those words to the list as they are found.

Day 2. Review the phonogram and the words listed on the chart paper from Day 1. Add new words that students have discovered from their reading. You may want to add a few longer (multisyllabic) words to the list to show students that knowledge of the word family can help them figure out even longer and more difficult words. Read through the list once or twice.

At this point, students have some familiarity with the word family. However, most of their reading of the phonogram has been with words in isolation. You want students to get practice in reading the phonograms in the context of authentic text. So this is the point to introduce a poem or two that contains the targeted word family words. Here is where this book comes in handy. Put the poem(s) on chart paper, the chalkboard, or an overhead transparency.

Read through each poem several times until students can read it on their own. The rhyme, rhythm, and repetition make each poem easy for students to learn to read. Then, begin to draw students' attention to individual words and word parts in the poem. Have them point to individual words and words that contain particular elements, such as certain letters and blends at the beginning of the words, word families, repeated words, rhyming words, high-frequency words, and others.

You may want to use a "window" device that allows students to isolate individual words or word parts in a poem. An easy way to make a "window" or "word whopper" is to buy an old-fashioned fly swatter and cut out a rectangular window in the screen part. Students then hold the window by the handle and manipulate it so that only an individual word or word part can be shown through the window.

Students can also underline individual words with colored markers and write individual words from the poem on magic slates as you draw their attention to them. Finally, students can be given copies of the poem(s) to take home and read to their families and friends (e.g., Lucky Listeners).

Day 3. The third and final step in this instructional routine begins at the end of the second day. Through repeated reading of the poems, students begin to learn how poems are constructed. Then, having read a poem or two that contains a targeted phonogram, ask students to create their own poem using the phonogram for the following day. It can be a simple two-, three-, or four-line poem, but it needs to contain words of the targeted word family. The list of words on the chart from Day 1 can be a great help to students.

For many students, such a task can be difficult. Thus, we encourage you to provide as much help as possible in order for them to be successful. Students can work in groups of two or three to make their poems. They can work with older students from another class or with adult volunteers in your room. Students are even encouraged to work with their parents or other family members to write their poems. This is a great way to involve parents in their children's reading and writing development. We don't even care if, at first, students' partners do most of the work. Eventually, and quickly in most cases, the students catch on and become poets on their own. Regardless of how the poem is made, the expectation is for students to come into class on the third day of the routine with a simple poem in their hands. (Several of the poems published throughout this book were written by young readers!)

Students transfer their poems to chart paper or onto blank overhead projector transparencies. The writing itself is good practice for students to internalize the phonograms they are working on. Once this is done, the poems are hung around the room (if they are written on chart paper) and phonics instruction for the third day essentially becomes a poetry festival. Imagine what your classroom might look like! If you have 24 students in your room, you may have 8 to 12 poems hanging proudly around your classroom!

Then, in groups, students move around the classroom, reading and rereading the poems that have been authored by their classmates. The author has the privilege of reading the poem first. Then, as on the previous day, each poem is read chorally once or twice and then individually by those students who might want to give it a try on their own. Students' attention is drawn to the key words in the poem, and then the group moves on to the next poem.

You can see that by the end of the session, students should have pretty well mastered the targeted word family. But even more, by the end of this session, students will have developed a greater appreciation for poetry and the work of poets, for they have been involved in the creation of poetry to share with others in a very authentic format. The poems can later be collected, typed, copied, and bound in the form of a class-authored book for each student to read later and celebrate his or her own authorship of published poetry!

Throughout this routine, other phonogram phonics activities can be taking place as well. Most notably, games (e.g., Bingo) give students practice in identifying words that contain the targeted and other phonograms.

Every poem in this book has an accompanying additional activity sheet. Each of these sheets contains a word bank that includes significant words from the accompanying poem. There are also blanks for teachers and students to add their own words to the bank. Copy the Word Bank Black Line Master form on page 170 and write in the words for a particular poem (those from the activity sheet itself and those chosen by the teacher and students). Then duplicate the filled-in sheet so that every child has a copy of the word bank. The words can be cut into individual word cards and practiced throughout the next several days. Word games, such as Match, in which two identical sets of words are turned over and students take turns trying to find the various matched pairs, are easy to do with the word bank cards. Students could also be asked to put the words into alphabetical order.

But perhaps the most beneficial activity to engage students in with their word banks are word sorts. Students take their deck of word cards and sort them into categories called out by the teacher or by fellow classmates (e.g., "Sort your words into two piles—those words that belong to the *at* word family and those that don't"; "Sort your words into two piles—words that refer to people and words that don't"). With each word sort, not only are students getting practice on the words they are learning but they are also getting opportunities to examine each word from a different perspective with each sort, thereby engaging in deep analysis of each word and developing greater control of various features of the words.

On the activity sheet, we also provide suggested categories for sorting. Forward slashes around individual letters or letter patterns (e.g., /at/) refer to the "sound of" the letter or letter pattern.

Also on each activity sheet are five cloze sentences. Cloze sentences are sentences in which a key word from the word bank has been deleted. Students determine the key word by using the meaningful context surrounding the deleted word. This gives students practice in using another beneficial cue for figuring out words—meaning and syntax. The cloze sentences should be copied onto chart paper or the chalkboard, or made into a transparency so that all students can see the sentences as they are figured out by the students. In some cases, the cloze sentences are strung together to form a simple story.

Finally, certain activity sheets contain other instructional suggestions, such as creating another version of the poem, reading a related book, or brainstorming and examining words related to a topic. All the activities in this sheet provide students with extra practice and exposure to words they need to learn.

The key element in this instructional routine, however, is the focus on poetry that contains the targeted word families. As students read, write, and read poems that contain words with key phonograms, they are learning phonics in an intensive, systematic, authentic, meaningful, and engaging way—a way that will ensure efficient and masterful learning, a way that will lead to fascination about the written word, and a way that will lead students to more reading and more writing. The foundation upon which this approach is built are the phonogram poems that are contained in this book.

Regardless of how you may use these poems with your students—to learn phonics or simply to have some fun with poetry, or both—we wish you much success in helping your students become successful and lifelong readers.

References

Adams, M. (1990). *Beginning to read: Thinking and learning about print.* Cambridge, MA: MIT Press.

Clymer, T. (1963/1996). The utility of phonic generalizations. *The Reading Teacher, 16/50*, 252–258/182–185.

Cunningham, P. (1995). *Phonics they use.* New York: HarperCollins.

Fry, E. (1998). The most common phonograms. *The Reading Teacher, 51,* 620–622.

Gaskins, I. W., Downer, M. A., Anderson, R. C., Cunningham, P. M., Gaskins, R. W., & Schommer, M. (1998). A metacognitive approach to phonics: Using what you know to decode what you don't know. *Remedial and Special Education, 9,* 36–41.

Gaskins, I. W., Ehri, L. C., Cress, C., O'Hara, C., & Donelly, K. (1997). Procedures for word learning: Making discoveries about words. *The Reading Teacher, 50,* 312–327.

Goswami, U., & Bryant, P. (1990). *Phonological skills and learning to read.* East Sussex, UK: Erlbaum.

Johnston, F. R. (1999). The timing and teaching of word families. *The Reading Teacher, 53,* 64–75.

Johnston, F. R. (1999, December). *The utility of phonic generalizations: Let's take another look at Clymer's conclusions.* Paper presented at the annual meeting of the National Reading Conference, Orlando, FL.

Stahl, S. A. (1992). Saying the 'P' word: Nine guidelines for exemplary phonics instruction. *The Reading Teacher, 45,* 618–625.

Trieman, R. (1985). Onsets and rimes as units of spoken syllables: Evidence from children. *Journal of Experimental Child Psychology, 39,* 161–181.

Vacca, J. L., Vacca, R. T., & Gove, M. K. (1995). *Reading and learning to read.* New York: HarperCollins.

Always Rain

Rain, rain, always rain.
A little more rain and I'll go insane.
Stuck in the house can be a big pain.
Rain, rain, always, rain.

—Timothy Rasinski

Word Bank Words

Always Rain

rain	more	big
pain	and	insane
store	stand	dig

Ways to Sort (categories):

① /ān/, ② /ore/, ③ /ig/, ④ /and/, ⑤ words that are actions, ⑥ words with silent letters (letters whose normal sounds are not heard)

Cloze Sentences:

1. Andy likes to _____ holes in the backyard.
2. I went to the _____ to buy more bread.
3. Bears _____ pandas are cute animals.
4. After the _____ we played in the puddles.
5. One _____ point and we will win the game.

Other Activities:

Read *Cloudy with a Chance of Meatballs* by Judi Barrett (ISBN: 0689306474, Atheneum).

Beef Stew Hot,
Beef Stew Cold

Beef stew hot, beef stew cold,
beef stew in the pot
five days old.
Come eat my beef stew
although it's not very new.
Will many come to eat it?
Probably just a few.

—Timothy Rasinski

Word Bank Words

Beef Stew Hot, Beef Stew Cold

cold	old	new
stew	pot	hot
gold	blew	spot

Ways to Sort (categories):

① /ot/, ② /old/, ③ /ew/, ④ words that contain a consonant blend (hint: old, gold, and cold have consonant blends) ⑤ words that could refer to the weather, ⑥ words that describe things, ⑦ pairs of words that are opposites

Cloze Sentences:

1. The cold wind _____ against my cheeks.
2. Silver and _____ are used to make jewelry.
3. Some people like soup; I prefer _____.
4. In winter the weather is often _____.
5. On my birthday I got a brand _____ bike.

Other Activities:

Brainstorm, discuss, and list other opposites:

old- new   up- ___   alive- ___   beautiful- ___

cold- hot   fat- ___   dog- ___   win- ___

day- ___   inside- ___ nice- ___   early- ___

Bikes

Bikes are to ride
All of the day
Places to go
So far away

Sidewalks and paths
Places to stray
Riding a bike
Is a great way to play.

—Greg Reagan

Word Bank Words

Bikes

day	play	places
away	way	sidewalks
stray	bikes	paths

Ways to Sort (categories):

① /ā/ words, ② plural words/ words ending with s (e.g., bikes), ③ words that contain a consonant blend, ④ /ī/ words

Cloze Sentences:

1. The _____ cat was looking for a home.
2. Let's _____ tag at recess.
3. The opposite of "night" is _____.
4. We can ride our _____ to the park.
5. There are many _____ we can visit.

Bob

-id
-ob

Diddle diddle dumpling, my son Bob
Skinned his knee and began to sob.
Gave him a pickle and corn on the cob.
Diddle diddle dumping, my son Bob.

—Timothy Rasinski

16

Word Bank Words

Bob

Bob	sob	my
corn	him	his
horn	try	Jim

Ways to Sort (categories):

① /ob/, ② /ī/, ③ /orn/, ④ /im/, ⑤ words that are names, ⑥ words that refer to boys or men, ⑦ words that have words within them (hint: *or* in *corn* and *horn; is* in *his*)

Cloze Sentences:

1. Jim has a trombone. My _____ is a trumpet.
2. I planted _____ in my garden this year.
3. When Jim fell off his bike he began to _____.
4. Be sure to always _____ your hardest.
5. When my mother is angry she calls me Robert, not _____.

Other Activities:

1. Make a list of nicknames and their formal versions:

   Bob-Robert   Bill-_____

   Jim-James   Barb-_____

2. Write another version of this poem using a name other than Bob.

Call the Doctors

Jack is ill and Jill is sick.
I'm not kidding, it's no trick.
Call Doctor William
Call Doctor Rick
Get them here mighty quick.
Through the valley, over the hills
Tell them we need their medical skills.

—Timothy Rasinski

Word Bank Words

Call the Doctors

ill	sick	quick
Jill	trick	call
fill	Rick	all

Ways to Sort (categories):

① /ill/, ② /ick/, ③ /all/, ④ words that make new words when the first letter is removed

Cloze Sentences:

1. I will _____ up the car with gas.
2. I can _____ you on April Fools' Day.
3. Please _____ me if you need a ride.
4. A word that means the same as "sick" is _____.
5. The opposite of "slow" is _____.

Other Activities:

1. Read Elleen Christelow's *Five Little Monkeys Jumping on the Bed* (similar "call the doctor" theme) (Clarion Books, 1989).
2. Read *The Lady with the Alligator Purse* by Nadine Westcott (Little, Brown, 1990).

Chili in a Pot

Chili in a pot,
cook it up hot,
I'm really hungry,
so give me a lot!

—**Karen McGuigan Brothers**

Word Bank Words

Chili in a Pot

chili	hungry	pot
hot	cook	so
potter	crook	also

Ways to Sort (categories):

① /ot/, ② /ook/ as in *cook*, ③ /ē/, ④ /ō/, ⑤ words with 2 syllables, ⑥ words that refer to "professions" or "jobs" that people may have to make money, ⑦ words that refer to food or eating

Cloze Sentences:

1. I like my chili good and _____.
2. The _____ crook stole bread and jam.
3. Don't touch that pot—it's much too _____.
4. I am _____ hungry—I need to eat now!
5. My dad loves to cook, _____ does my mom.

Other Activities:

Explain analogies and do a few.

hot : pot :: hat : pat

(hot is to pot as hat is to pat)

so : also :: ways: _____

pot : potter :: hat : _____

The Choo Choo Train

The choo choo train
does chug and chug,
up the hill like a little bug.
If it stops,
it will need a tug,
that choo choo train
that chugs and chugs.

—Timothy Rasinski

Word Bank Words

The Choo Choo Train

chugs	bug	tug
hill	will	stops
shops	chill	buggy

Ways to Sort (categories):

① /ug/, ② /ill/, ③ /op/, ④ words with a consonant digraph /sh/ or /ch/, ⑤ words that end in /s/, ⑥ words that have words within them (e.g., *hug* in *chugs*)

Cloze Sentences:

1. My sister loves to _____ for clothes.
2. When I was a baby I was pushed in a _____.
3. That _____ looks pretty steep.
4. I found a _____ in my garden.
5. Step on the brake and the car _____.

Other Activities:

Brainstorm and categorize words that refer to trains and railroads.

The Crab

On the beach I found a crab,
I gave him just a little jab.
He moved so slow
I didn't know
my finger he would grab!

—Karen McGuigan Brothers

Word Bank Words

The Crab

crab	jab	grab
slow	know	so
mow	crow	cab

Ways to Sort (categories):

① /ab/, ② /ō/, ③ words that begin with a consonant blend, ④ words that refer to animals, ⑤ words with silent letters, ⑥ words that have words within them

Cloze Sentences:

1. In the summer my dad will _____ the lawn.
2. Do you _____ where my toys are?
3. Another name for a taxi is a _____.
4. When my brother is in a bad mood I call him a _____.
5. He cries when I _____ him on the shoulder.

Dark, Dark
and Stormy Night

It was a dark dark
and stormy night.
Even the cat
was filled with fright.
I felt a cold chill
when I heard the first scream.
Opened my door
Happy Halloween!

—Timothy Rasinski

Word Bank Words

Dark, Dark and Stormy Night

dark	night	fright
cat	chill	filled
bark	rat	silly

Ways to Sort (categories):

① /ark/, ② /ill/, ③ /ight/, ④ /at/, ⑤ words that are names of animals,
⑥ words that are connected with fear or being afraid

Cloze Sentences:

1. Cats meow and dogs _____.
2. My _____ friend often acts like a clown.
3. It was very _____. Not even the moon was out.
4. Before the long drive, I _____ up the car with gas.
5. The cool night air gave me a _____.

Other Activities:

Brainstorm and web Halloween words or words associated with another holiday.

Drew

There was a young boy named Drew
Whose library books were overdue.
He kept on forgetting
It was highly upsetting
Because his fine simply grew and grew!

—Belinda Zimmerman

Word Bank Words

Drew

Drew	grew	boy
fine	book	there
toy	mine	took

Ways to Sort (categories):

① /ew/, as in *few*, ② /oy/, ③ /ine/, ④ /ook/, ⑤ words that contain consonant blends, ⑥ words that refer to things, ⑦ words that can have more than one meaning (e.g., *drew, fine, mine*)

Cloze Sentences:

1. My friend Drew _____ to be six feet tall!
2. My toys are _____, next to my bed.
3. I _____ my dog to school today.
4. The books on the table are _____, not yours.
5. _____ is a new boy in my school.

A Duck Named Chuck

There once was a duck named Chuck
who wanted to drive a truck.
I wished him good luck,
but he got stuck in the muck.
Now poor Chuck is the
duck with no luck.

—Lisa M. Dimling

Word Bank Words

A Duck Named Chuck

Chuck	truck	duck
drive	poor	he
she	hive	dive

Ways to Sort (categories):

① /uck/, ② /īve/, ③ words with /ē/, ④ words that refer to people, ⑤ words beginning with /d/, ⑥ words beginning with /h/, ⑦ words that begin with a consonant blend

Cloze Sentences:

1. He sold his car and bought a new _____.
2. Don't go near that _____, the bees look angry.
3. _____ Chuck, he just crashed his truck.
4. New cars are fun to _____.
5. She loves to _____ into the pool.

Other Activities:

Read *Make Way for Ducklings* by Robert McCloskey (ISBN: 0670451495, Viking).

Earthquake!

Oh my, for heaven's sake!
I think we're having a big earthquake.
The house it shakes,
there's cracks in the floor.
Oh wait, it's just an elephant
knocking at my door.

—Timothy Rasinski

Word Bank Words

Earthquake!

sake	take	poor
earthquake	floor	knocking
shakes	door	having

Ways to Sort (categories):

① /ake/, ② /or/, ③ /ing/, ④ 2-syllable words, ⑤ words that contain other words within them

Cloze Sentences:

1. The _____ caused the house to tremble.
2. Mom gently _____ me to wake me up.
3. The opposite of "rich" is _____.
4. Who is _____ at the door?
5. We are _____ a bake sale at school.

The Eating Clan

-am
-an
-ink

Hot dogs, burgers, cheese and ham.
Bread and toast, jelly and jam.
Now for something cool to drink.
Pop that's red, lemonade that's pink.
My family is an eating clan.
Chew and swallow all we can.

—Timothy Rasinski

Word Bank Words

The Eating Clan

ham	drink	clan
jam	pink	can
Sam	think	fan

Ways to Sort (categories):

① /am/, ② /ink/, ③ /an/, ④ /ă/, ⑤ words that are things that can be swallowed

Cloze Sentences:

1. Sam's favorite book is *Green Eggs and* _____.
2. Lemonade is my favorite _____.
3. Toast tastes best with _____.
4. Sit by the _____ to cool off.
5. I _____ it might rain today.

Other Activities:

1. Share the book called *Pig Out* (an "All Aboard Reading" book by Portia Aborio, published by Grosset & Dunlap). This is a fun rebus book.
2. Share the chant "Junk Food" by Sonja Dunn (Heinemann). Dunn suggests that children get into a circle and take turns chanting their favorite junk food selection. If the children "forget" or are unable to think of a junk food to share, they can simply clap to maintain the rhythm of this delightful chant.

Emily

-as (s)
-y(ē)

There once was a girl named Emily.
She came from a respectable family.
They all went to mass
and Sunday School class
and never acted up or got silly.

—Emily Rutzky, Justin Parsons,
Cody White, Sara Tebeau, and Danielle Sommers

Word Bank Words

Emily

and	came	class
mass	all	went
stand	tallest	sent

Ways to Sort (categories):

① /and/, ② /all/, ③ /ass/, ④ /ent/, ⑤ words that contain a consonant blend, ⑥ words with double letters, ⑦ words with a /ĕ/

Cloze Sentences:

1. _____ of my friends are in my class.
2. My mother _____ me to the store to buy milk.
3. I am the _____ girl in my family.
4. Soldiers have to _____ at attention.
5. Emily _____ I are best friends.

Fast Crab

A lazy cranberry-colored crab
sunned itself on a granite slab.
A dinner I thought I might easily nab
But it scurried so fast it was hard to grab.

—Timothy Rasinski

38

Word Bank Words

Fast Crab

crab	slab	nab
granite	itself	it
hard	card	hardware

Ways to Sort (categories):

① /ab/, ② /it/ (hint: *granite* has the sound of *it*), ③ /ard/, ④ words with 2 syllables, ⑤ words that contain a consonant blend, ⑥ words with a silent *e*

Cloze Sentences:

1. I bought a hammer at the _____ store.
2. I paid for _____ with my own money.
3. Poker is a type of _____ game.
4. I caught a hermit _____ on the beach.
5. Granite is a very _____ rock.

Other Activities:

Brainstorm and list other animals and objects that can be found on a beach.

The Frog

I sat upon a log
and watched a big green frog.
By and by
he caught a fly,
then hopped right into the bog.

—**Karen McGuigan Brothers**

40

Word Bank Words

The Frog

log	frog	fly
by	big	hopped
stopped	wig	hog

Ways to Sort (categories):

① /og/, ② /ig/, ③ /ī/, ④ /op/, ⑤ words that refer to animals, ⑥ words that are actions, ⑦ words that end in /t/

Cloze Sentences:

1. I saw a _____ today by the pond.
2. One frog _____ right up to me.
3. I will wear a _____ for Halloween.
4. My _____ brother is two years older than me.
5. Should I put another _____ on the fire?

Get Out of Bed!

You'd better get out of bed
and grab your big red sled.
I looked out and found
there's snow on the ground
and it's nearly up to my head!

— Karen McGuigan Brothers

Word Bank Words

Get Out of Bed!

bed	sled	head
snow	out	better
glows	shout	petted

Ways to Sort (categories):

① /ed/ (hint: *head* has the *ed* sound), ② /out/, ③ /et/, ④ /ō/, ⑤ words that contain a /t/, ⑥ words that are actions

Cloze Sentences:

1. The _____ is almost one inch deep.
2. My dog loves to be _____.
3. It's so cold my _____ hurts.
4. I love how the moon _____ at night.
5. When I'm tired I head straight to _____.

Other Activities:

Brainstorm and list activities to do when it snows.

A Good Deed

If you want to do a good deed,
then give the birds some seed.
It's very nice
when there's snow and ice
to help fill their every need.

—Karen McGuigan Brothers

Word Bank Words

A Good Deed

seed	deed	nice
ice	fill	need
slice	bleed	still

Ways to Sort (categories):

① /eed/, ② /ice/, ③ /ill/, ④ words that begin with /s/, ⑤ words with double letters, ⑥ words that contain a consonant blend, ⑦ words that are things that can be touched

Cloze Sentences:

1. The air is calm; the wind is _____.
2. My drink is warm. I _____ some ice.
3. Plant a _____ and watch it grow.
4. Cut your finger and it will _____.
5. It is always nice to do a good _____.

Other Activities:

Think of and list all the names that contain *ill* (e.g., *Jill, Bill, William, Millie, Will, Hillary*)

There once was a princess named Grace.
She had a very lovely face.
But she was fickle and coy
Around every boy,
And became a royal disgrace.

—Belinda Zimmerman

Word Bank Words

Grace

grace	face	she
had	very	and
sad	graceful	race

Ways to Sort (categories):

① /ace/, ② /ad/, ③ /ē/, ④ /ă/, ⑤ words that refer to people, ⑥ words that contain 2 syllables

Cloze Sentences:

1. My sister is charming and _____.
2. When I am sad it shows on my _____.
3. I _____ a feeling that I would win the race.
4. I am _____ careful when I cross the street.
5. _____ had to take the bus to school today.

I call my grandpa "Pap."
I like to sit on his lap.
He reads me good books,
and sometime he cooks,
and usually takes a long nap.

—Karen McGuigan Brothers

Word Bank Words

Grandpa

lap	nap	books
looks	takes	like
make	bike	cap

Ways to Sort (categories):

① /ap/, ② /ook/, ③ /ake/, ④ /ike/, ⑤ words with a silent e, ⑥ words that describe things a person can touch

Cloze Sentences:

1. When I am tired I often take a _____.
2. It _____ like we will win this game.
3. I _____ to ride my bike.
4. The wind blew my _____ right off my head!
5. My mom can _____ the best pizzas.

Other Activities:

Make analogies:

bake : make :: bike : Mike (bake is to make as bike is to Mike)

map : sleep :: cap: _____

read : books :: ride: _____

The Greedy Boy

-are (air)   -ine
-end   -oy

"Rain or shine
I want what's mine,"
so said the greedy boy.

"My game, my bike, my ball of twine,
my basket full of toys.

I don't care
I will not share,"
he said to the bitter end,
and so with despair, no one would dare
to make this boy their friend.

—Timothy Rasinski

50

Word Bank Words

The Greedy Boy

mine	twine	share
shine	care	friends
spend	basket	bitter

Ways to Sort (categories):

① /ine/, ② /are/ as in *air*, ③ /end/, ④ 2-syllable words, ⑤ words with 2 letters that represent one sound (digraphs), ⑥ words that help make friends

Cloze Sentences:

1. That brand new bike is _____.
2. Tam and Tim are best _____.
3. I like to _____ time with my grandma.
4. She keeps her twine in a _____.
5. My brother and I _____ everything.

Other Activities:

Read *"I Don't Care!" Said the Bear* by Colin West to the class (ISBN: 076360125X, Candlewick).

Hank's Prank

Happy Hank played a prank
on his mom and dad.
They didn't like it,
he got spanked.
Now Happy Hank is sad!

—Timothy Rasinski

Word Bank Words

Hank's Prank

Hank	dad	glad
prank	sad	mad
spanked	tank	happy
bank		

Ways to Sort (categories):

① /ank/, ② /ad/, ③ words that contain a consonant blend, ④ /h/

Cloze Sentences:

1. Hank's parents did not like the _____.
2. I went to the _____ to deposit money.
3. I am named after my _____.
4. When my hamster was sick I felt _____.
5. The boy named _____ played a prank.

Other Activities:

Share the book *Tricking Tracy* (a Tadpoles book by Rigby) with the children. This easy reader is about a young girl who likes to play pranks. This is a good text to read aloud or to use in guided reading.

Harry

My old friend Harry is a little scary
when I see him drive his car.
Old and weary, he named it Mary.
I know it won't go far.

—Timothy Rasinski

Word Bank Words

Harry

Harry	weary	far
scary	baby	old
Mary	car	gold

Ways to Sort (categories):

① /ary/ as in *airy*, ② /ar/ words, ③ words that end with /ē/,
④ words with 2 syllables, ⑤ words that contain a consonant blend
(hint: *ld* is a consonant blend)

Cloze Sentences:

1. The _____ movie gave us a fright.
2. A _____ cat is called a kitten.
3. The opposite of "near" is _____.
4. The leprechaun had a pot of _____.
5. Dad sold his _____ and got a van.

Other Activities:

Design and describe your dream car or a car that Harry might like.

Hickory Dickory Chick

Hickory dickory dock,
the chick ran to the clock.
The clock struck ten,
she found the hen.
Hickory dickory dock.

—Timothy Rasinski

Word Bank Words

Hickory Dickory Chick

hickory	dickory	chick
ten	hen	dock
tent	pick	rock

Ways to Sort (categories):

① /ick/, ② /ock/, ③ /en/, ④ 3-syllable words, ⑤ words with a consonant digraph (e.g., ck, ch), ⑥ words that contain /d/

Cloze Sentences:

1. The boat will stop at the _____.
2. I love to camp and sleep in a _____.
3. That _____ is too heavy to pick up.
4. The final score was _____ to six.
5. After the chicks went by, I saw the mother _____.

Other Activities:

Rewrite the poem, substituting another animal for chick (e.g., dog, horse, pig, etc.).

Hickory Dickory Dink

-ack -ink
-ick -or

Hickory dickory dink.
The duck swims in the sink.
His name is Jack.
He loves to quack.
Hickory dickory dink.

—Timothy Rasinski

Word Bank Words

Hickory Dickory Dink

duck	dink	Jack
dickory	sink	quack
pink	stink	sack

Ways to Sort (categories):

① /ink/, ② /ack/, ③ words beginning with /d/, ④ words containing an /s/, ⑤ words that end in /k/, ⑥ words that refer to living things

Cloze Sentences:

1. _____ and Jill went up the hill.
2. Chickens cluck and ducks _____.
3. Jill's favorite color is _____.
4. My mother packed my lunch in a _____.
5. Jack washed his hands in the _____.

Other Activities:

Write a group poem using the same model (e.g., Hickory Dickory Jack . . .).

Hickory Dickory Shine

-ick
-ine
-ock

Hickory dickory dock.
Fireflies flew into the clock.
The clock struck nine,
they started to shine.
Hickory dickory dock.

—Timothy Rasinski

Word Bank Words

Hickory Dickory Shine

nine	shine	clock
started	flew	they
wine	rock	star

Ways to Sort (categories):

① /ine/, ② /ock/, ③ /ar/, ④ words that contain a consonant blend, ⑤ words that are things that can be touched, ⑥ words that have words within them

Cloze Sentences:

1. Some say that cats have _____ lives.
2. We went inside when it _____ to rain.
3. My parents have _____ with their dinner.
4. Did you see how bright the stars _____?
5. I like to listen to _____ and roll music.

Other Activities:

Make a list of objects and actions:

stars-shine   cars-_____

dogs-bark   swimmers-____

balls-roll   _____ -sing

grass- _____

My dear friend Jack was feeling ill.
Seems he had a little chill.
Jill could tell
he wasn't well.
So they quickly ran down the hill.

—**Karen McGuigan Brothers and Timothy Rasinski**

Word Bank Words

Hills, Chills, and Ills

hill	ill	friend
Jill	chill	Jack
tell	well	they

Ways to Sort (categories):

① /ill/ words, ② /ell/ words, ③ words that contain a consonant digraph (2 consonants, 1 sound), ④ words that refer to people, ⑤ words that could be places

Cloze Sentences:

1. Did Jack take _____ up the hill?
2. Let me _____ you a story.
3. Wear your sweater today or you may get a _____.
4. _____ were the best of friends.
5. I love to play with my _____ Jack.

Other Activities:

Read the traditional *Jack and Jill* rhyme.

Holly Kristine

There was a girl named Holly Kristine.
She was never ever stingy or mean.
Instead she was nice,
Ate chicken soup with rice,
And she always helped her mother to clean.

—**Holly Dawe and Belinda Zimmerman**

Word Bank Words

Holly Kristine

mean	nice	rice
clean	mother	chicken
sister	sick	never

Ways to Sort (categories):

① /ean/, ② /ice/, ③ /ick/, ④ words that refer to living things, ⑤ words that describe people, ⑥ 2-syllable words, ⑦ words that have words within them

Cloze Sentences:

Note: These cloze sentences go together to form a brief story.
1. My sister always makes me _____ our room.
2. I think she is _____ to make me do all the work.
3. My mother _____ makes her work at all.
4. It makes me feel _____.
5. Why can't my sister be _____ ?

Other Activities:

Try writing a similar poem using a boy's name in place of Holly Kristine.

How Special I Am!

If I were a crow, I'd wear a big bow
so people would know how special I am.

If I were a deer, I'd stand up and cheer
so people would hear how special I am.

If I were a goat, I'd wear a red coat
so people would note how special I am.

If I were a lark, I'd glow in the dark
and folks would remark how special I am.

If I were a bear, I'd send up a flare
to brightly declare how special I am.

But I'm not a crow who wears a big bow;
and I'm not a deer who shouts out a cheer;
and I'm not a goat who wears a red coat;
and I'm not a lark who glows in the dark;
and I'm not a bear, I don't have a flare.

I am just me; there's only one me
and it's plain to see how special I am!

—Karen McGuigan Brothers

Word Bank Words

How Special I Am!

bow	crow	coat
goat	dark	remark
below	parka	boat

Ways to Sort (categories):

① words that end in /ō/, ② words that contain /ō/, ③ /oat/, ④ /ark/, ⑤ words that end in a vowel sound, ⑥ 2-syllable words, ⑦ words that refer to clothing

Cloze Sentences:

1. When it's cold I either wear my coat or my _____.
2. The airplane flew above and _____ the clouds.
3. A large _____ was tied on the front of the gift.
4. Once the sun went down, the sky became _____.
5. My _____ can cross the lake in two minutes!

Other Activities:

Create a group story on chart paper using all or most of the word bank words.

I Love to Eat Apples

I love to eat apples
and more than a few.
Early in the morning
when they're covered in dew.
I love to eat apples,
when they're red and they're new.
Crisp and sweet,
what a delight to chew.

—Alison Drews

68

Word Bank Words

I Love to Eat Apples

few	dew	chew
sweet	eat	more
neat	feet	store

Ways to Sort (categories):

① /ew/ as in few, ② /ēt/, ③ /ore/, ④ words that begin with a consonant blend, ⑤ words that refer to food, ⑥ words that contain a silent letter (e.g., store, neat)

Cloze Sentences:

1. The _____ often glistens on the leaves in the morning.
2. I bought a few apples at the _____.
3. Three _____ days until my birthday!
4. I love to eat _____ treats.
5. After running a mile, my _____ are sore.

Other Activities:

Make a list of opposite or contracting pairs:

sweet-sour	feet-_____	you-_____
meat-_____	more-_____	him-_____
few-_____	mow-_____	mom-_____

The Ice Cream Man

The ice cream man rings his bell.
He has some frozen treats to sell.
Chocolate or cherry,
or even strawberry,
they look as good as they smell.

—Karen McGuigan Brothers

70

Word Bank Words

The Ice Cream Man

bell	sell	smell
man	treats	cream
swell	ran	dream

Ways to Sort (categories):

① /ell/, ② /ē/, ③ /an/, ④ words that contain a consonant blend, ⑤ words that refer to things that can be eaten, ⑥ words with two of the same letters (e.g., sell, treats)

Cloze Sentences:

1. Ice cream is one of my favorite _____.
2. I _____ all the way home from school today.
3. My dad thinks that sweet treats are _____.
4. Our trip to Disney World is a _____ come true.
5. I love the _____ of cookies in the oven.

Other Activities:

Write a short story using the words from the word bank.

Icky Sticky Prickly Pet

Icky sticky prickly pet.
Porcupines for dinner,
Have you had yours yet?

I'm not very hungry.
I don't think I'll eat.
Porcupines for dinner
Isn't much of a treat.

—Timothy Rasinski

Word Bank Words

Icky Sticky Prickly Pet

icky	vet	eat
sticky	pet	treat
prickly	yet	meat

Ways to Sort (categories):

① /ick/, ② /et/, ③ /eat/, ④ words that refer to living things, ⑤ words beginning with /p/, ⑥ words that contain a consonant blend

Cloze Sentences:

1. Vegetarians do not eat _____.
2. Cotton candy is a _____ treat.
3. Porcupines make _____ pets.
4. The _____ made our cat feel better.
5. I have not opened my presents _____.

Other Activities:

1. Have children create (draw) a real or imaginary prickly pet. The children should include a list of describing words (or some sentences) that tell about their picture of the pet.
2. During guided reading, have children read *Hedgehog Is Hungry* (a beginning PM Reader book from Rigby).

If

If you don't cry
and if you don't pout,
I'll take you fishing
and you can catch trout.

—**Karen McGuigan Brothers**

Word Bank Words

If

pout	trout	cry
can	take	you
try	bake	out

Ways to Sort (categories):

① /out/, ② /ake/, ③ /y/ = ī, ④ words that contain a consonant blend, ⑤ words that describe actions by children when they are not happy, ⑥ words with /t/

Cloze Sentences:

1. Always _____ to do your best.
2. My mom likes to _____ cookies and cakes.
3. When the sun shines, I _____ play outside.
4. _____ me out to the ball game.
5. When will _____ play with me?

Other Activities:

Brainstorm and list other names of fish and sea creatures.

If My Shoes Could Talk

-all
-ay
-ip

If my shoes could talk
I guess they would say
they've done a lot
of things today.

They walked along
the garden wall;
they jumped and ran
to catch a ball,

They hopped and shuffled,
they danced and skipped,
they pedaled my bike,
they almost tripped!

They clung to my skateboard
through the sidewalks of town
and walked through a puddle
with mud all around.

If my shoes could talk
I know what they would say.
They've had a very
busy day!

—Karen McGuigan Brothers

Word Bank Words

If My Shoes Could Talk

say	today	wall
ball	skip	trip
slippers	tallest	may

Ways to Sort (categories):

① /ay/, ② /ip/, ③ /all/, ④ words that contain a consonant blend, ⑤ words with 2 syllables, ⑥ words with double letters, ⑦ words that have words within them

Cloze Sentences:

1. _____ I am seven years old!
2. Skippy is the _____ in his classroom.
3. I hope we can take a _____ to the zoo.
4. My dad got _____ for his birthday.
5. I _____ miss school tomorrow if I still feel ill.

77

Jack's Lunch

Jack likes to pack
his lunch in a sack.
He's very well fed
on jelly and bread
with cookies for a snack.

—Karen McGuigan Brothers

78

Word Bank Words

Jack's Lunch

pack	snack	sack
jelly	lunch	well
belly	munch	sells

Ways to Sort (categories):

① /ack/, ② /unch/, ③ /ell/, ④ words that refer to food or eating, ⑤ words that begin with /s/, ⑥ words with 2 syllables

Cloze Sentences:

1. I like to eat peanut butter and _____ sandwiches.
2. My dad _____ cars.
3. I have carrots in my lunch for a _____.
4. When I eat too much candy, I don't feel _____.
5. Did you ever eat your _____ for breakfast?

Other Activities:

Do a survey of favorite lunch foods. Display the results as a set of bar graphs.

Just Try

A bird can fly
up in the sky.
A baby can cry
when he's not dry.
You can ask why
if you're not too shy,
and if you think you can't
just try.

—Karen McGuigan Brothers

Word Bank Words

Just Try

fly	sky	baby
cry	ask	thinks
my	mask	blink

Ways to Sort (categories):

① /ī/, ② /ask/, ③ /ink/, ④ words that contain a consonant blend, ⑤ words that describe things done on or in one's head, ⑥ words with the /k/ sound

Cloze Sentences:

1. I like to fly in the _____.
2. Mom _____ the baby will cry when she leaves.
3. _____ your mother if you can play with me.
4. Tom has a great _____ for Halloween.
5. I have never seen my brother _____.

Other Activities:

Brainstorm and list /ink/ words. Then try to write sentences that contain at least 2 /ink/ words.

Justin

-ed   -out
-it   -us

There once was a guy named Justin
whose boss told him he better start hustlin'
He stomped and he pouted
and finally he shouted,
I quit! There's no doubt about it!

—Justin Parsons

Word Bank Words

Justin

boss	pouted	shouted
quit	stomped	about
toss	bit	kitten

Ways to Sort (categories):

① /oss/, ② /out/, ③ /it/, ④ words with 2 syllables, ⑤ words in the past tense (*ed* endings), ⑥ words with 2 of the same letter, ⑦ words that describe actions people do when they are mad

Cloze Sentences:

1. The supervisor is my _____.
2. The coach _____ at his players.
3. We have two pets—a dog and a _____.
4. My little sister _____ when she didn't get her way.
5. I like to talk _____ books after reading them.

The Kitten

There once was a young girl named Erin
who found a kitten named Karen.
Her friend said, "No fair!
Unless there's a pair
that kitten you'll have to be sharin'!"

—Erin Gragson and Sara Tebeau

Word Bank Words

The Kitten

kittens	fair	pair
that	her	girl
sat	perfect	sitter

Ways to Sort (categories):

① /air/, ② /er/, ③ /at/, ④ words with 2 syllables

Cloze Sentences:

1. Erin is my baby _____ tonight.
2. My friend and I make a funny _____.
3. Our cat had four _____.
4. _____ girl is very smart.
5. Are you going to the county _____ tonight?

Other Activities:

Brainstorm and list other words associated with cats and kittens.

Ladybug

A ladybug is under the rug,
I think she's fast asleep.
Take her out and give her a hug,
and she'll always be yours to keep.

—Karen McGuigan Brothers

Word Bank Words

Ladybug

rug	asleep	think
hug	keep	fast
deep	last	sink

Ways to Sort (categories):

① /ug/, ② /eep/, ③ /ink/, ④ /ast/, ⑤ words that contain a consonant blend, ⑥ words with vowels that say their names (long vowels)

Cloze Sentences:

1. Please wash the dishes in the _____.
2. Everyday my dad gives me a _____.
3. I fell fast _____ while watching TV.
4. We dug a _____ hole in the backyard.
5. Can I _____ the dollar I found today?

Other Activities:

Brainstorm and list other names of bugs.

Manners

Please don't snore
when you take a nap.
Did you like the play?
Then you ought to clap.
And when you say hello,
be sure to doff your cap.
You see, learning manners
can be a snap.

—**Timothy Rasinski**

Word Bank Words

Manners

snore	nap	clap
snap	play	take
clay	chores	snake

Ways to Sort (categories):

① /ore/, ② /ap/, ③ /ay/, ④ /ake/, ⑤ /sn/, ⑥ /cl/, ⑦ words that are sounds people make

Cloze Sentences:

1. I can _____ when I finish my chores.
2. Be careful—that turtle can _____.
3. I hope they _____ at the end of the play.
4. When I hear snoring, I know my dad is taking his _____.
5. In art class I made a snake out of _____.

Other Activities:

Make a list of rules for good manners in school and at home.

Milk and Cookies

When you have your milk and cookies
do you sometimes like to dunk?
Do you eat them at the table,
or take them to your bunk?
Do you store them in the cupboard,
or hide them in a trunk?
When you dip them in your milk,
do you ever lose a hunk???
(I hate when that happens . . .
it turns my milk to "gunk!")

—Karen McGuigan Brothers

Word Bank Words

Milk and Cookies

dunk	bunk	trunk
like	eat	hide
bike	sunk	treat

Ways to Sort (categories):

① /unk/, ② /eat/, ③ /ike/, ④ /ī/, ⑤ words that contain a consonant blend,
⑥ words that have words within them

Cloze Sentences:

1. My brother and I have _____ beds.
2. My friends and I like to play "_____ and Go Seek."
3. An elephant can have a long _____.
4. Did you _____ all your lunch?
5. Brownies are my favorite _____.

Other Activities:

Survey the class on their favorite drinks. Display the results as a bar graph.

Murphy the Cat

I have a cat who's white and gray.
He always seems to be in my way.
At the end of my bed he likes to lay,
and with my hair he'll often play.
I love my cat. What more can I say?
We'll be friends till our dying day.

—Sandy Sika

Word Bank Words

Murphy the Cat

gray	play	cat
always	white	more
today	matter	score

Ways to Sort (categories):

① /at/, ② /ay/, ③ /ore/, ④ words with 2 syllables, ⑤ words that contain a consonant blend, ⑥ color words

Cloze Sentences:

1. _____ be kind to your pet.
2. My cat never listens, no _____ what I say.
3. Our team won, but I forgot the _____.
4. It rained yesterday, but _____ is nice.
5. Recess is always a good time to _____.

Other Activities:

Brainstorm and list different kinds of cats (e.g., lions, tigers, etc.).

My Daddy

My daddy's name is Bob,
he works all day at his job,
But on Saturday
he stays home to play
and cooks hot dogs and corn on the cob.

—Karen McGuigan Brothers

Word Bank Words

My Daddy

Bob	job	Saturday
name	play	home
game	Monday	dome

Ways to Sort (categories):

① /ob/, ② /ay/, ③ /ame/, ④ /ome/, ⑤ words that are days of the week,
⑥ words with a silent *e*

Cloze Sentences:

1. On _____ I get to sleep in because there is no school.
2. My brother _____ plays games with me.
3. Bob's full _____ is Robert.
4. A large round _____ sits on top of the United States Capitol.
5. I live in a two-story _____.

Other Activities:

List the days of the week. Model how each day can be decoded by its parts.

My Dear Aunt Jean

My dear Aunt Jean,
how she loves to clean
her house from bottom to top.
With a bucket and mop, you'll see what I mean.
She never wants to stop.

—Timothy Rasinski

Word Bank Words

My Dear Aunt Jean

Jean	lean	stop
clean	top	hop
mean	mop	drop

Ways to Sort (categories):

① /ean/, ② /op/, ③ words that begin with /m/, ④ words that are actions,
⑤ words that contain a consonant blend

Cloze Sentences:

1. On Saturday, we will _____ the car.
2. The opposite of "nice" is _____.
3. The "bunny _____" is a type of dance.
4. The red sign tells us to _____.
5. Try not to _____ the football.

Other Activities:

Write a letter to Aunt Jean to convince her to clean your room.

My Dog, Tag

I have a dog named Tag
who plays with a paper bag.
I open it wide
and he gets inside
and gives his tail a wag.

—Karen McGuigan Brothers

98

Word Bank Words

My Dog, Tag

tag	bag	wide
inside	tail	dog
sailor	jog	mail

Ways to Sort (categories):

① /ag/, ② /ide/, ③ /og/, ④ /ail/, ⑤ words that refer to living things,
⑥ 2-syllable words

Cloze Sentences:

1. I like to play _____ with my friend.
2. My brother is a _____ in the Navy.
3. Our dog likes to chase his _____.
4. My friend sent me a letter in the _____.
5. It was so cold we had to _____ to warm up.

Other Activities:

Brainstorm, list, and categorize words related to dogs.

My Friend Chester

My friend Chester is a real pest.
He pesters his sister and
his sister's guest.

He pesters his family
never gives them any rest

Oh, my friend Chester is a real pest.

—Timothy Rasinski

Word Bank Words

My Friend Chester

pest	best	sister
guest	Chester	never
rest	pester	clever

Ways to Sort (categories):

① /est/ words, ② words ending with /er/ (e.g., Chester) ③ words that are people,
④ 2-syllable words

Cloze Sentences:

1. A flea can be quite a _____.
2. Chester is my _____ friend.
3. You are tired and need to _____.
4. We invited Amy to be our _____ for dinner.
5. To be smart is to be _____.

Other Activities:

In *Phonics They Use*, Patricia Cunningham (1995) suggests playing a variation of the game show Wheel of Fortune. Words from the poem "My Friend Chester" (or any poem) may be used. Here are Cunningham's (p. 159) suggestions for playing The Wheel:

Remind the children that it is possible to problem-solve through a word even if we cannot sound it all out, if we think about what makes sense and whether it has any parts we do know in the right places. Game rules:

1. Teacher selects several words from the poem.
2. Players guess all letters without considering if they are consonants or vowels.
3. They must have all letters filled in before they can say the word (encourages learning to spell and attention to common spelling patterns).
4. They win paperclips instead of prizes.
5. Teacher writes the category for the game on the board and draws blanks for each letter.
6. A child begins by asking, "Is there a...?" If child guesses correctly, letter is filled in and child receives a paperclip for each time that letter occurs. Child may continue to guess until he "misses." Write incorrect letter guess on board.
7. When all letters are filled in, someone may guess. The one who correctly guesses earns 5 bonus paperclips. The child with the most paperclips at the end is the winner!

My Friend Shum

My friend Shum loved chewing gum.
Guess you could say he was my chewing chum.
Chewed while he sang,
chewed while he hummed,
chewed in the band while he played his drum.

—Timothy Rasinski

Word Bank Words

My Friend Shum

gum	chum	drum
sang	band	while
rang	sand	mile

Ways to Sort (categories):

① /um/, ② /ang/, ③ /and/, ④ /ile/, ⑤ words associated with songs and music, ⑥ words that make new words when the first letter is removed

Cloze Sentences:

1. My sister plays the flute in the _____.
2. I could run a _____ in the sand.
3. We cleaned our rooms _____ our mother made lunch.
4. On Christmas day the church bells _____.
5. Susan _____ while I played the drum.

Other Activities:

Brainstorm and list other versions of the first line of this poem, (using children's names from the class (e.g., "My friend Tim just loves to swim...").

My Mom's Car

My mom's car is really clunky
but she calls it her Mister Spunky.
It smells like a skunk.
It's just a piece of junk.
It should be driven by a monkey.

—Timothy Rasinski

Word Bank Words

My Mom's Car

clunky	spunky	junk
smell	car	mister
tell	star	sister

Ways to Sort (categories):

① /unk/, ② /ell/, ③ /ar/, ④ /is/, ⑤ 2-syllable words, ⑥ words that refer to people, ⑦ words that could describe people

Cloze Sentences:

1. I love the _____ of my mom's perfume.
2. My sister is the _____ of the show.
3. Clunky old cars end up in the _____ yard.
4. I couldn't _____ where the smell was coming from.
5. My brother and _____ can make me laugh.

Other Activities:

Brainstorm, list, and categorize words associated with cars.

My Uncle Pete

My Uncle Pete really loves to eat
whenever he has an itchin'.
Meats and beets and sweet-tooth treats,
whatever's in the kitchen.

—Timothy Rasinski

Word Bank Words

My Uncle Pete

eat	seat	pItcher
meats	itching	beets
treats	kitchen	sweet

Ways to Sort (categories):

① /eat/, ② /ch/, ③ words with 2 syllables, ④ plural words,
⑤ words that are things that can be eaten

Cloze Sentences:

1. It is fun to get _____ on Halloween.
2. I like to _____ pizza and ice cream.
3. It is my turn to clean up the _____.
4. My brother Pete is our team's _____.
5. The chocolate sundae tasted _____.

Other Activities:

1. Have children brainstorm a list of "Meats and Beets" foods and then "Sweet-Tooth Treats." Have them select foods from each list to create a balanced meal for Uncle Pete.
2. Have children create a cartoon of Uncle Pete going to visit his doctor. The children can use speech bubbles to capture the dialogue of what the doctor and Uncle Pete say when Pete steps onto the scale.

My Wagon

I've got the best wagon
I know that it's true.
I just finished painting it
red, white, and blue

It's a Fourth of July wagon
It flies our great flag.
My dog even salutes
when he makes his tail wag.

—Timothy Rasinski

Word Bank Words

My Wagon

true	blue	flag
white	wagon	just
bite	must	termites

Ways to Sort (categories):

① /uel/, ② /ag/, ③ /ust/, ④ /ite/, ⑤ color words, ⑥ 2-syllable words, ⑦ words with consonant blends, ⑧ words with silent letters

Cloze Sentences:

1. Sue is a _____ blue friend.
2. _____ are insects that like to eat wood.
3. We made it to the game _____ in time.
4. I _____ remember to do my homework.
5. The sun is out and the sky is _____.

Other Activities:

Brainstorm, list, and categorize words associated with the Fourth of July.

Ned and Fred

Ned and Fred
rode their sled
down the hill
and hit the shed.
They saw the doctor,
she sent them to bed.
Now chicken soup
is all they're fed!

—Meredith Maurer

Word Bank Words

Ned and Fred

Ned	shed	down
Fred	bed	now
sled	fed	flower

Ways to Sort (categories):

① /ed/ words, ② words with /ow/ as in *now*, ④ words that are things that are normally found outdoors, ⑤ words with a consonant blend

Cloze Sentences:

1. Ned and _____ rode their sled.
2. Mom keeps her tools in the _____.
3. I _____ my puppy food from a can.
4. Ted fell _____ and scraped his knee.
5. The rose is a lovely _____.

Other Activities:

Share the poem "Let's Go Coasting" by Nona Keen Duffy from *Poetry Place Anthology* (Instructor Books, p. 51).

The Nest Builder

A bird built a nest
and it was simply the best
of all of the nests in the tree.
In his nest which was the best
he could lay down and rest
or watch a little TV!

—Karen McGuigan Brothers

Word Bank Words

The Nest Builder

nest	best	tree
down	all	rest
fall	clowns	free

Ways to Sort (categories):

① /est/, ② /all/, ③ /own/ as in *down,* ④ /ē/, ⑤ words that contain a consonant blend (hint: *rest* contains a constant blend), ⑥ words with short vowel sounds

Cloze Sentences:

1. I hope that bird doesn't _____ out of his nest.
2. Of all the circus people, I like the _____ best.
3. I'm tired—let's _____ for a while.
4. My mom saw three nests in that _____.
5. The clown falls _____ a lot.

Other Activities:

Read to children the book *A House Is a House for Me* by Mary Ann Hoberman (ISBN: 0140503943, Viking). Discuss different types of homes.

Oh My Gosh, Josh!

-ail -oor
-ear -osk
-ell -ug

My trike ran over the kitty's tail,
I tripped and spilled Mom's scrubbing pail,
I bumped the lamp and down it fell,
"Oh my gosh, Josh!" Mom said with a yell.

I wrote on the wall with my pretty red crayon,
I made mud pies in my mother's best pan,
the sandbox sand got all over my head,
"Oh my gosh, Josh!" my mother said.

I spilled the sugar all over the floor,
my peanut butter sandwich stuck to the door,
I gave my dog a bubble bath wash,
and when Mom found out she said, "Oh my gosh,
Josh!"

I painted some letters on Mom's new rug.
She yelled when she saw it, then gave me a hug.
"I love you, Mom" the letters read clear.
"Oh my gosh, Josh," she said with a tear.

—Karen McGuigan Brothers

Word Bank Words

Oh My Gosh, Josh!

tail	pail	fell
yell	hug	clear
rail	bug	ear
head	love	fail

Ways to Sort (categories):

① /ail/, ② /ell/, ③ /ear/, ④ /ug/, ⑤ words that are parts of a body,
⑥ words associated with being happy, ⑦ words associated with being sad

Cloze Sentences:

1. I love to get a _____ from my mom.
2. Please don't _____ in the library.
3. After the storm, the sky is _____.
4. I cleaned my room with rags and a _____ of water.
5. My dad tells me always to use my _____.

Oh My, Please Don't Cry

Oh my, please don't cry.
Won't you give it one more try?
When things don't go as
you'd like them to,
don't feel bad
and don't feel blue.
Just try once more
and you'll succeed.
I believe in you,
yes indeed.

—Timothy Rasinski

Word Bank Words

Oh My, Please Don't Cry

cry	try	bad
succeed	indeed	feel
need	sad	peel

Ways to Sort (categories):

① /ī/, ② /eed/, ③ /ad/, ④ /eel/, ⑤ /ē/, ⑥ 2-syllable words

Cloze Sentences:

1. Some people _____ when they feel sad.
2. Don't slip on that banana _____ .
3. I _____ a new bike.
4. Always try to _____ at whatever you do.
5. I _____ good today!

Other Activities:

Make a list of "feeling" words by asking students to describe how they feel today.

Old King Stan

Old King Stan
was a stout old man
and a stout old man at that.
He called for his cake,
and sweet cookies just baked,
and he called himself too fat.

—Timothy Rasinski

Word Bank Words

Old King Stan

king	Stan	man
stout	called	old
shout	gold	sold

Ways to Sort (categories):

① /an/, ② /out/, ③ /old/, ④ words that contain a consonant blend, ⑤ words that refer to people, ⑥ words that are actions

Cloze Sentences:

1. The king is getting _____ and gray.
2. I _____ my bike to Stan.
3. _____ coins are very expensive.
4. My teacher _____ my mom on the phone.
5. That _____ old man can eat a lot.

Other Activities:

Rewrite the first two lines of "Old King Stan" using different names and rhymes. (e.g., "Old King Sam loved jelly and jam . . .").

Ouch!

I stubbed my toe on a rock
and put a hole in my sock.
My mom said "too bad,"
My dad said "so sad,"
but the clock just kept saying "tick-tock."

—Karen McGuigan Brothers

Word Bank Words

Ouch!

rock	sock	dad
sad	toe	just
flock	Joe	must

Ways to Sort (categories):

① /ock/, ② /ad/, ③ /ast/, ④ /ō/, ⑤ words with 2 letters that make one sound, ⑥ words that end in a consonant blend

Cloze Sentences:

1. I am so _____ I feel like crying.
2. My _____ has a hole in the toe.
3. Our friend _____ missed school today.
4. Elvis is the King of _____ and roll.
5. _____ two more dollars and I can buy a new bike.

Other Activities:

Read and perform poems from the collection *Toes in My Nose* by Sheree Fitch (ISBN: 1563971275, Boyds Mill).

Phillip's Trip

Down the steps did Phillip trip.
Seems he sort of lost his grip.
Slide slide slide and slip
Not much fun was Phillip's trip.

—Timothy Rasinski

Word Bank Words

Phillip's Trip

trip	drip	Phillip
grip	slide	phone
slip	glide	

Ways to Sort (categories):

① /ip/, ② /ide/, ③ words beginning with r blends (e.g., trip) ④ words beginning with s blends (e.g., steps), ⑤ words containing /f/ sound

Cloze Sentences:

1. My family will take a _____ this summer.
2. It's hard not to _____ on the ice.
3. You can reach me by e-mail or _____.
4. I play on the _____ during recess.
5. The paper plane will _____ through the air.

Other Activities:

To give children more experience with the "-ip" chunk in meaningful context, read aloud the traditional tale of the *Three Billy Goats Gruff*. Children will enjoy acting this one out or performing a reader's theater for this story. Audience members can make and hold up signs that say "Trip-Trap, Trip-Trap, Trip-Trap" or say "Who's that trip-trapping over my bridge?" as each billy goat crosses the bridge.

123

Pickup Truck

Pickup truck, pickup truck,
I could drive all day
in my pickup truck.

Just cruise along,
never get stuck.
I could drive all day
in my pickup truck.

Fill it with chickens,
geese, or ducks,
I could drive all day
in my pickup truck.

Give a ride to
Chip and Chuck.
They could ride all day
in my pickup truck.

Pickup truck, pickup truck,
I could drive all day
in my pickup truck.

—Timothy Rasinski

Word Bank Words

Pickup Truck

Chip	Chuck	drive
truck	day	ride
play	strong	ditch
hide		

Ways to Sort (categories):

① /ch/, ② /uck/, ③ /ide/, ④ /ay/, ⑤ words with /ī/, ⑥ words that contain a consonant blend, ⑦ words that make new words when the first letter is removed, ⑧ words that make words when the last letter is removed

Cloze Sentences:

1. Chuck drove the _____ into a ditch.
2. _____ and seek is a fun game to play.
3. I like to _____ my brother's bike.
4. Chip and Kip are _____. They can lift a truck!
5. When I get older, I want to _____ a car.

Other Activities:

Read antiphonally with two groups of students. One group reads the refrain, "I could drive all day in my pickup truck."

Picky Ricky

Picky Ricky gets so sticky,
picking through his candy.
Picky Ricky looks so icky,
but he thinks it's dandy.

—Timothy Rasinski

Word Bank Words

Picky Ricky

picky	icky	bricks
Ricky	candy	and
sticky	dandy	sand

Ways to Sort (categories):

① /ick/, ② words that end with /ī/, ③ /and/and/andy/ words, ④ words beginning with a consonant blend, ⑤ words that make new words when the first letter is removed.

Cloze Sentences:

1. The taffy made his fingers _____.
2. The smart pig built a house of _____.
3. I like chocolate _____ vanilla ice cream.
4. I made a _____ castle by the sea.
5. _____ apples are sweet treats.

Other Activities:

Share the book *Picky Nicky* by Cathy East Dubowski and Mark Dubowski. This is a delightful rebus book with a related theme (an "All Aboard Reading" book published by Grosset & Dunlap).

Poor Frank!

He kept his money in a bank
in the cellar dark and dank.
He lost the key
and so said he,
"I'll have to open it with a crank."
Poor Frank.

—Karen McGuigan Brothers

Word Bank Words

Poor Frank!

bank	crank	Frank
dark	cellar	kept
market	basement	slept
nap		

Ways to Sort (categories):

① /ank/, ② /ar/, ③ words that mean the same thing, ④ /ept/,
⑤ 2-syllable words, ⑥ words that end in a consonant blend

Cloze Sentences:

1. I _____ like a baby last night.
2. The _____ room and creaky door made Frank feel jittery and jumpy.
3. My mom sent me to the _____ for milk.
4. John's shouting _____ me up last night.
5. I bought a savings bond at the _____.

Other Activities:

Brainstorm, list, and discuss other hand tools besides a crank

The Possum

The possum sat on a rail
eating apples from a pail.
If she should trip
or lose her grip
she'll hold on with her tail.

—Karen McGuigan Brothers

Word Bank Words

The Possum

tail	rail	trip
grip	hold	eating
singing	bold	tripping

Ways to Sort (categories):

① /ing/, ② /ail/, ③ /ip/, ④ /old/, ⑤ 2-syllable words, ⑥ words that make new words when the first letter is removed

Cloze Sentences:

1. The dog got his _____ caught in the door.
2. I hear my sister _____ in the shower.
3. Don't _____ over the dog.
4. Soldiers have to be brave and _____.
5. If you think you're tripping, _____ on to the railing.

Other Activities:

Brainstorm and list other wild animals.

The Queen Is In

Hail, all hail, the queen is in!
It's just my sister, the evil twin.
Whether it's playing cards
or in a swim,
it never fails, she has to win.

She is my sister,
my family kin,
but being around her
can make my head spin.

I call her queen,
without question or fail,
until I figure out
how to send her to jail.

—Timothy Rasinski

Word Bank Words

The Queen Is In

twin	win	fail
send	how	jail
bend	chow	sister

Ways to Sort (categories):

① /in/, ② /ail/, ③ /end/, ④ /ow/ as in *how*, ⑤ words with 2 letters that make one sound (digraph), ⑥ words that contain a consonant blend

Cloze Sentences:

1. A magician can make a metal spoon _____.
2. _____ is a good place for crooks.
3. Did you _____ your game?
4. When's _____? I'm hungry!
5. I hate to _____ any test.

Other Activities:

Read *The Pain and the Great One* by Judy Blume (ISBN: 0027111008, Simon and Schuster).

Rae

There was a little lady named Rae.
She had a most horrible day.
It was lightning and raining
so she started complaining,
"If it won't stop, I'll just run away!"

—Rae-Lin Jones, Justin Parsons, Holly Dawe,
Emily Hook, and Moriah Asefi

Word Bank Words

Rae

day	away	raining
stop	complaining	most
shopping	daylight	ghost

Ways to Sort (categories):

① /ay/, ② /op/, ③ /ain/, ④ /ost/, ⑤ /ing/, ⑥ words with 2 syllables, ⑦ words containing letters whose usual sounds are not heard

Cloze Sentences:

1. I love to hear scary _____ stories.
2. It has been _____ most of this cloudy day.
3. My dad asked me to _____ complaining.
4. My dog ran _____ yesterday.
5. In the fall and winter, we get fewer hours of _____.

Other Activities:

Read and reread the chant:

Rain rain go away,

Come again another day,

Little Johnny wants to play.

Rain rain go away.

I like to watch the rain.
It grows the corn and grain,
It rolls down the street
and wets my feet,
then goes right down the drain.

—Karen McGuigan Brothers

Word Bank Words

The Rain

rain	grain	street
feet	corn	grow
greets	horn	crow

Ways to Sort (categories):

① /ain/, ② /eet/, ③ /orn/, ④ /ow/ = ō, ⑤ words that begin with /gr/,
⑥ words that are objects or things

Cloze Sentences:

1. Wheat _____ gets turned into flour and bread.
2. The old _____ loves to eat my corn.
3. Always be careful when you cross a _____.
4. I hope to _____ six feet tall.
5. My mom _____ me at the door when I come home from school.

Other Activities:

Brainstorm, list, and discuss other items grown by farmers.

Rich

There was a clutzy kid named Rich
who tripped right into a big fat ditch.
He fell on his head.
They thought he was dead.
But all he needed was a stitch.

—Richard Fife and Eric Vaught

138

Word Bank Words

Rich

Rich	ditch	tripped
head	dead	fell
thread	fellow	clippers

Ways to Sort (categories):

① /ich/, ② /ip/, ③ /ed/, ④ /ell/, ⑤ words containing letters whose usual sounds are not heard (silent letters), ⑥ words containing a consonant blend, ⑦ words that are actions

Cloze Sentences:

1. Mom knows how to use a needle and _____.
2. My friend Sam _____ and hit his head.
3. My dad cut my hair with his set of _____.
4. My hair _____ to the ground when it was cut.
5. My friend Rich is a very good _____.

Silly Sam

I know who I am,
my mom calls me Silly Sam.
I'm tall and slim
with a happy grin
and my favorite foods are ham
and jam.

—Karen McGuigan Brothers

Word Bank Words

Silly Sam

Sam	favorite	tall
ham	jam	happy
hamster	clap	taller
pancakes		

Ways to Sort (categories):

① /am/, ② /all/, ③ /ap/, ④ words with 2 or 3 syllables, ⑤ words with a consonant blend, ⑥ words that are foods

Cloze Sentences:

1. _____ is a nickname for Samuel or Samantha.
2. I am _____ than Sam or Rich.
3. _____ your hands at the end of the play.
4. Give me _____ with plenty of syrup and I'll be happy all day!
5. Hamsters are my _____ pets.

Other Activities:

Survey class members for their favorite breakfast, lunch, and supper foods. Display the results as tables or bar graphs.

Sing and Shout

Hey get happy, let's sing and shout.
Don't feel sad, don't you dare pout.
Spring is near, the warm winds blow.
Won't be long before they melt the snow.
Then we'll play and dance about.
So let's be happy, let's sing and shout.

—Timothy Rasinski

Word Bank Words

Sing and Shout

shout	blow	snow
about	melt	feel
sleet	pelted	melted

Ways to Sort (categories):

① /out/, ② /ow/ = ō, ③ /ē/, ④ /elt/, ⑤ 2-syllable words, ⑥ past-tense words (words that end in *ed*), ⑦ winter weather words

Cloze Sentences:

1. The snow has _____; we can't ride our sleds.
2. The sleet _____ the roof and sounded like a drum.
3. It is so cold—_____ ten below zero!
4. We had to _____ to be heard over the sound of the heavy wind.
5. I _____ like playing in the snow today.

Other Activities:

Brainstorm, list, and categorize winter or spring time activities.

Ted

Diddle diddle dumpling, my son Ted
played all day on his sled.
Was so tired, went straight to bed.
Diddle diddle dumpling, my son Ted.

—Timothy Rasinski

Word Bank Words

Ted

Ted	sled	his
son	all	sister
Fred	ton	called

Ways to Sort (categories):

① /ed/, ② /all/, ③ /is/, ④ /un/, ⑤ 2-syllable words, ⑥ words that contain a consonant blend (hint: *sister* does not have a consonant blend), ⑦ people words

Cloze Sentences:

1. Fred and _____ are best friends.
2. Gosh, that is heavy. It must weigh a _____.
3. I am my father's _____.
4. Fred's _____ is a friendly girl.
5. Ted _____ his mother at work.

Other Activities:

Brainstorm and list activities that make a person tired.

That Cow

I'd like to ride that cow
if you could tell me how.
She is so high,
but I could try
if she would first take a bow.

—Karen McGuigan Brothers

Word Bank Words

That Cow

cow	how	high
try	tell	ride
bell	slide	fly
sky		

Ways to Sort (categories):

① /ow/ as in *cow*, ② words that end in /ī/, ③ /ell/, ④ /īde/,
⑤ words that contain /ī/, ⑥ words that refer to flying in an airplane

Cloze Sentences:

1. That cow _____ has a funny sound.
2. I'd like to learn to _____ a jet airplane.
3. Please tell me _____ much it costs to ride the bus.
4. I love to play on the _____ at recess.
5. On cloudless nights the _____ is full of stars.

Other Activities:

Brainstorm and list other farm animals.

That Old Cat

-at
-ay
-un

That old cat just likes to nap
in my house and on my lap.
He sleeps and sleeps and sleeps all day.
He's got to find another way to play.
Out in the yard he needs to run.
Now that's the way to have some fun.
That old cat just likes to nap
in my house and on my lap.

—Timothy Rasinski

Word Bank Words

That Old Cat

nap	lap	house
run	fun	cat
mouse	stop	awake

Ways to Sort (categories):

① /ap/, ② /ouse/, ③ /un/, ④ words with silent letters, ⑤ word pairs that are opposites or contrasts, ⑥ words that refer to animals

Cloze Sentences:

1. I live in an old _____.
2. My dad is tired and takes a _____ when he comes home from work.
3. Be sure to _____ and look before crossing the street.
4. It's _____ to play outdoor games.
5. My _____ loves to run and jump onto my lap.

Other Activities:

Read the book *The Napping House* by Audrey Wood (ISBN: 0152567089, Harcourt Brace).

Tim Tam

Tim Tam the painting man
loves to paint any way he can.
He'll paint your rooms.
He'll paint your walls.
All you need to do is give him a call.

—Timothy Rasinski

Word Bank Words

Tim Tam

man	all	Tim
can	call	him
	walls	trim

Ways to Sort (categories):

① /an/, ② /all, ③ /im/, ④ words that refer to males, ⑤ words that make new words when the first letter is removed

Cloze Sentences:

1. The gingerbread man said, "Catch me if you _____."
2. There is no such thing as the boogie _____.
3. It is not kind to _____ people names.
4. _____ Tam is the painting man.
5. The barber gave Tim's hair a _____.

Other Activities:

Compare "Tim Tam" to *Dan the Flying Man* (a storybox reader from the Wright Group). Compare the two characters, Tim Tam and Dan. Have children note the similar language and word families.

Toys Galore

I had a dream the other night,
a happy dream, not even a fright.
Seems I lived inside a store
that had a name like "Toys Galore."

Don't get me wrong, I had a chore
to test those toys in that store.
When I finished, I'd get some more,
so many toys I was getting sore.

I had that dream the other night
to tell the truth, it was a fright.

—Timothy Rasinski

Word Bank Words

Toys Galore

chore	store	night
dream	name	fright
steam	same	came

Ways to Sort (categories):

① /ore/, ② /ight/, ③ /eam/, ④ /ame/, ⑤ words that contain a consonant blend, ⑥ words with silent letters

Cloze Sentences:

1. My big _____ at home is to carry out the trash.
2. I don't like dreams that give me a _____.
3. At _____ we play flashlight tag.
4. My brother and I have the same last _____.
5. When water boils it makes _____.

Other Activities:

Brainstorm, list, and sort students' favorite toys. Chart the children's favorites using a bar graph.

A Turkey Named Jim

Gobble gobble gobble, a turkey named Jim
happens to be awfully slim.
Works out daily in the turkey gym.
Not a Thanksgiving turkey,
this turkey named Jim.

—Timothy Rasinski

Word Bank Words

A Turkey Named Jim

Jim	slim	gym
turkey	this	out
stout	mister	shout

Ways to Sort (categories):

① /im/ (includes *gym*), ② /is/, ③ /out/, ④ words with 2 syllables, ⑤ words that refer to people, ⑥ words that could describe a person, ⑦ words with /er/ (includes *turkey*)

Cloze Sentences:

1. The opposite of slim is _____.
2. Tim and _____ are twin brothers.
3. Some people like chicken; I like _____.
4. I keep trim by working out in my _____.
5. Please don't _____. You're too loud!

Other Activities:

Make a list of other foods often eaten on Thanksgiving. Use the words to make a list poem.

Uncle Jake

My Uncle Jake just loves to bake
in his pastry store.
Cookies, bread, and lots of cakes
and other treats galore.

—Timothy Rasinski

Word Bank Words

Uncle Jake

Jake	snake	more
bake	store	chore
cakes	galore	take

Ways to Sort (categories):

① /ake/, ② /or/, ③ words with "s" blends (e.g., snake), ④ words that refer to living things

Cloze Sentences:

1. Washing windows can be quite a _____.
2. We went to the _____ to buy milk and cookies.
3. My pet _____ is beginning to shed its skin.
4. May I have some _____ ice cream?
5. Red Riding Hood took _____ to her Granny.

Other Activities:

1. Share *Along Comes Jake* (Set F Sunshine book from the Wright Group), which can be used to further reinforce the /ake/ word family.
2. Have children convert "Uncle Jake" into a rebus poem, inserting their own illustrations for the nouns in the poem. Examples: *store, cookies, bread, cakes, treats.*
3. Read *Kate Skates* (An "All Aboard Reading" book published by Grosset & Dunlap) for more experience with /ake/ words in a meaningful context.

Vacation Things

Reading and sleeping on hot summer days,
Painting and singing and putting on plays,
Kicking and running and jumping for fun,
Finding and asking how things are done,
Fishing and playing at the cool blue lake,
Dreaming and eating sweet ice cream cake,
Playing with all my neighborhood friends,
Hoping that summer never ends.

—Laurel Rowe

Word Bank Words

Vacation Things

reading	playing	lake
dreaming	plays	cake
eating	days	sleeping

Ways to Sort (categories):

① /ing/, ② /āl/, ③ /ake/, ④ words with /ē/ (e.g., reading), ⑤ words with /ē/ (e.g., sleeping)

Cloze Sentences:

1. I love _____ good books.
2. _____ sports is good exercise.
3. We have a boat on the _____.
4. My birthday is in four _____.
5. I like _____ late on the weekends.

Other Activities:

1. Read *It Looked Like Spilt Milk*. Using one's imagination to "read the clouds" is a lovely way to spend a summer vacation day!
2. Have the children write journal entries about fun warm-weather activities or events.

What's in That Pot?

Get a little, get a lot.
Put it all in a pot.
Cook it up, nice and hot.
Set it down, on that spot.
What do you have,
what have you got,
sitting there in that pot?
Is it soup? Maybe yes. Maybe not.

—Timothy Rasinski

Word Bank Words

What's in That Pot?

pot	got	it
lot	not	sitting
hot	get	
spot	set	

Ways to Sort (categories):

① /ot/, ② /et/, ③ /it/, ④ words that make new words when spelled in reverse order

Cloze Sentences:

1. Don't touch the stove—it's very _____ .
2. My popular brother has a _____ of friends.
3. Do you see the bird _____ in the tree?
4. Mom asked me to _____ the table.
5. Hawaii is a sunny vacation _____ .

Other Activities:

1. Share the book *Cooking Pot* (Set G Sunshine book by the Wright Group), which has a very similar "story line" and similar language.
2. Play a game with the children called "What's in That Pot?" Similar to the traditional game Twenty Questions, the children try to guess what is in the teacher's pot by asking questions that can be answered with a "yes" or a "no" from the teacher. The teacher records the questions in the form of statements on chart paper. For example: "Yes, it is bigger than a ruler," "No, it is not furry," and so on. After 10 to 20 statements are recorded, the children may specifically guess the item. For example, "Is it a book?" "Is it candy?" and so on.

William

William is my neighbor.
he has a willow tree.
It grows up on a hilltop
and billows in the breeze.

We laugh until we're silly
as we play up on the hill.
We go home when it's chilly
or when his mom calls "Bill."

—Colleen Kelly

Word Bank Words

William

William	billows	Bill
willow	silly	tree
hilltop	chilly	breeze

Ways to Sort (categories):

① /ill/, ② /ē/, ③ /ō/, ④ 2-syllable words, ⑤ words that contain a consonant blend or digraph

Cloze Sentences:

1. A cool _____ feels nice on a hot day.
2. I told a _____ joke.
3. _____ is a nick name for William.
4. We climbed the old oak _____.
5. The air is _____ in the Fall.

Other Activities:

1. Share the book *William's Doll* by Charlotte Zolotow with the children. Discuss whether the William in the story could be the same one as in the poem.
2. Brainstorm a list of "famous Williams" or "Bills."
3. Introduce children to the *Little Bill* children's book series by Bill Cosby.

Most Common Phonograms
(Word Families)

Other Phonograms

Index of Poems

169

Word Bank Black Line Master

Write the word bank words from the activity sheet following each poem. Add other words chosen by yourself and the students. Make a copy of the completed word bank for each student. Have students cut the word bank into individual word cards and sort the words into categories that represent various features found in the words.
